Doctors

Julie Murray

Abdo
MY COMMUNITY: JOBS
Kids

abdopublishing.com

Published by Abdo Kids, a division of ABDO, PO Box 398166, Minneapolis, Minnesota 55439.
Copyright © 2016 by Abdo Consulting Group, Inc. International copyrights reserved in all countries.
No part of this book may be reproduced in any form without written permission from the publisher.

Printed in the United States of America, North Mankato, Minnesota.

052015

092015

THIS BOOK CONTAINS
RECYCLED MATERIALS

Photo Credits: iStock

Production Contributors: Teddy Borth, Jennie Forsberg, Grace Hansen

Design Contributors: Candice Keimig, Dorothy Toth

Library of Congress Control Number: 2014958398

Cataloging-in-Publication Data

Murray, Julie.
 Doctors / Julie Murray.
  p. cm. -- (My community: jobs)
ISBN 978-1-62970-912-3
Includes index.
1. Doctors--Juvenile literature.   I. Title.
617--dc23
                    2014958398

Table of Contents

Doctors

Some doctors work in offices.

Others work in hospitals.

Doctors help people who are sick.

Doctors look in our ears.

They listen to our hearts.

They look in our mouths.

Jose says, "Ahhhhhh."

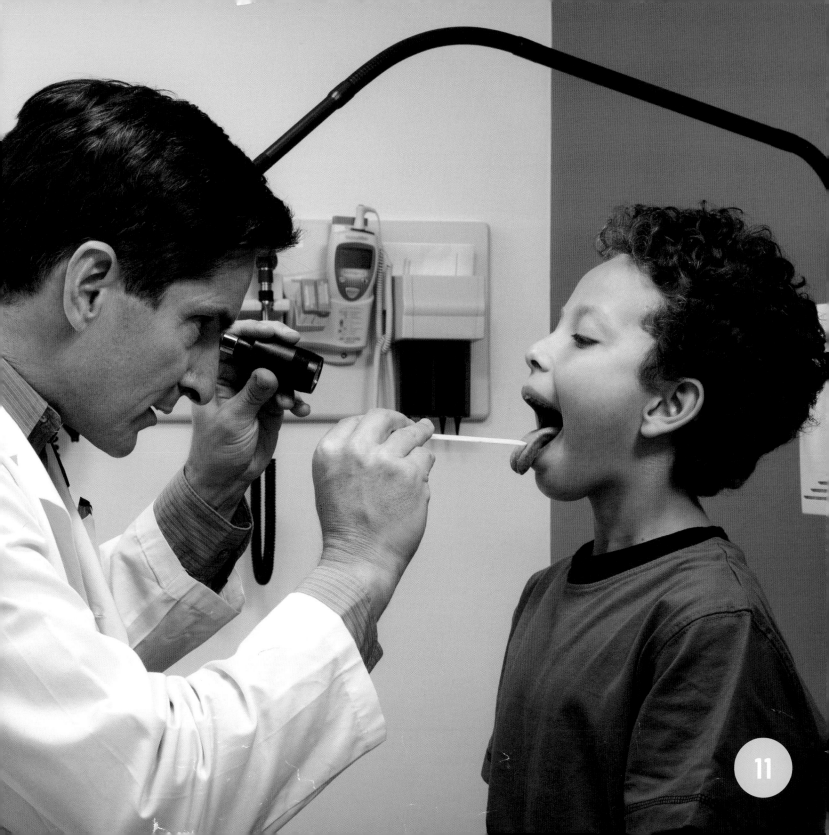

Sometimes they give us **medicine**.

Sometimes they give us shots.

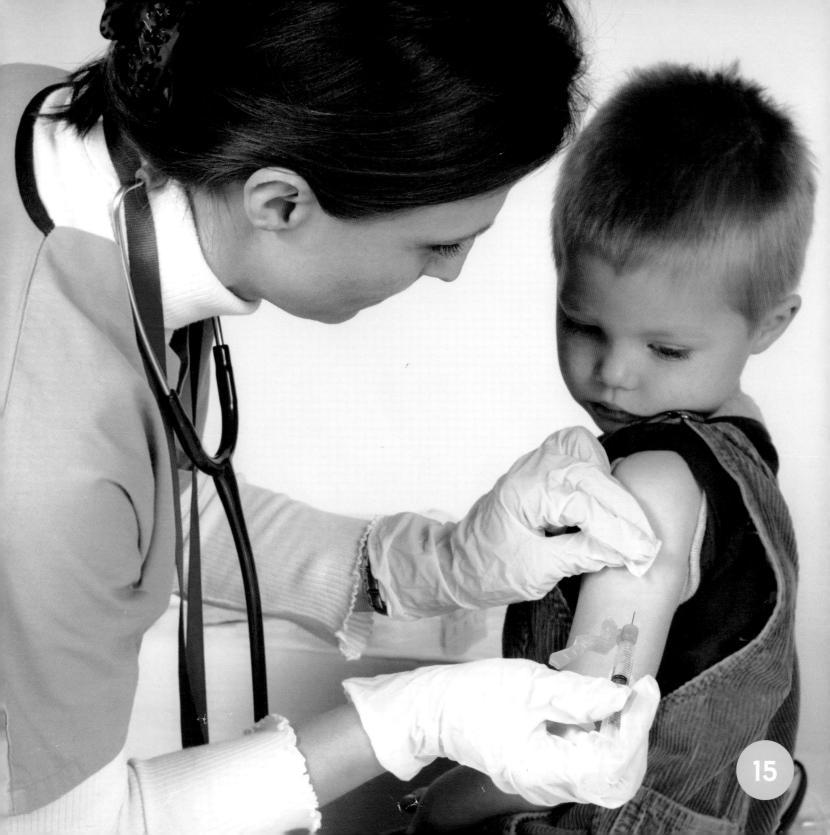

Doctors also look at X-rays.

They fix broken bones.

We go to the doctor for checkups. This keeps us healthy.

What does your doctor do?

A Doctor's Tools

blood pressure cuff

stethoscope

otoscope

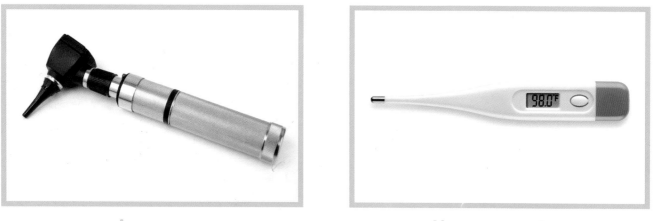

thermometer

Glossary

hospital
a place where sick or hurt people go to get better. Doctors and nurses work at hospitals.

office
a place to visit a family doctor for checkups.

medicine
what a doctor gives to people to help them feel better.

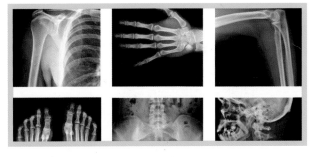

X-ray
a picture used to help a doctor figure out a problem inside the body.

Index

abdokids.com

Use this code to log on to abdokids.com and access crafts, games, videos, and more!

Abdo Kids Code:
MDK9123